ART at HOME

This book belongs to:

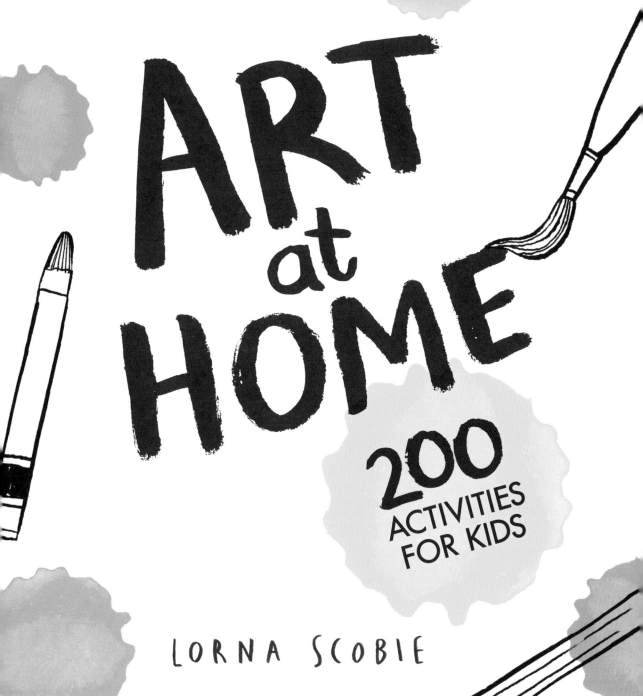

ART at HOME

200 ACTIVITIES FOR KIDS

LORNA SCOBIE

Hardie Grant

BOOKS

Welcome to Art at Home!

In this book you will find 200 activities chosen from the *365 Days* series, to inspire you to get creative. You will draw, paint, be inspired and have fun!

The most important thing to remember is that there is absolutely no wrong way to do these activities. This is YOUR book! Have a look at what the task suggests but feel free to create in whatever way you like – just go for it!

Often the drawing has been started for you, or an example is shown. Some activities will make you feel so relaxed that you will almost lose track of time! Others will ignite your interest in art and challenge your thinking.

Explore, enjoy and be as imaginative as you can!

Tip: Look out for hints and tips along the way!

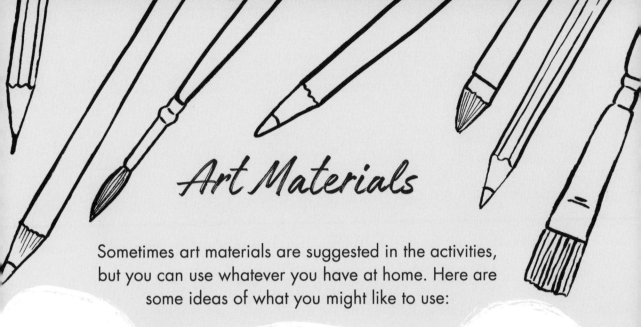

Art Materials

Sometimes art materials are suggested in the activities, but you can use whatever you have at home. Here are some ideas of what you might like to use:

Pencils
For drawing.

Colouring pencils
For drawing in colour.

Crayons (wax pastels)
For making thick marks.

A pencil sharpener
To keep your pencils lovely and sharp.

Paints
Perhaps also a palette so you can mix your colours.

Felt-tip pens
For adding bold colour to your art.

Brushes
Try all shapes and sizes.

Coloured paper
For creating collages.

Scissors
For cutting paper.

Tip: Ask a grown-up for help when you are using scissors.

Glue
Or a glue stick.

Progress Chart

You can do the activities in any order you like.
Circle them here as you finish them!

1	2	3	4	5	6	7	8	9	10
11	12	13	14	15	16	17	18	19	20
21	22	23	24	25	26	27	28	29	30
31	32	33	34	35	36	37	38	39	40
41	42	43	44	45	46	47	48	49	50
51	52	53	54	55	56	57	58	59	60
61	62	63	64	65	66	67	68	69	70
71	72	73	74	75	76	77	78	79	80
81	82	83	84	85	86	87	88	89	90
91	92	93	94	95	96	97	98	99	100

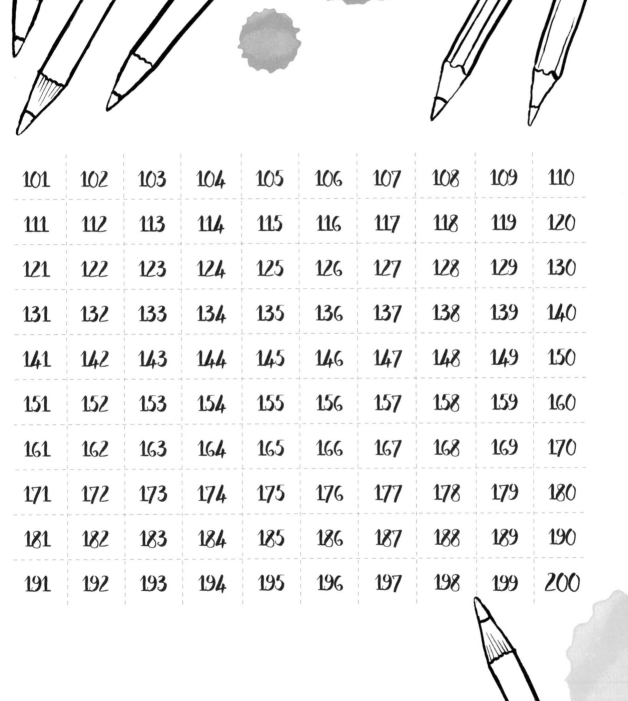

101	102	103	104	105	106	107	108	109	110
111	112	113	114	115	116	117	118	119	120
121	122	123	124	125	126	127	128	129	130
131	132	133	134	135	136	137	138	139	140
141	142	143	144	145	146	147	148	149	150
151	152	153	154	155	156	157	158	159	160
161	162	163	164	165	166	167	168	169	170
171	172	173	174	175	176	177	178	179	180
181	182	183	184	185	186	187	188	189	190
191	192	193	194	195	196	197	198	199	200

Tip: You could also colour in the pencils!

1

A colour wheel can be used to see which colours look good together. Colours found next to each other on the wheel often go well. Colours opposite each other can look bold and striking together. Create your own colour wheel below.

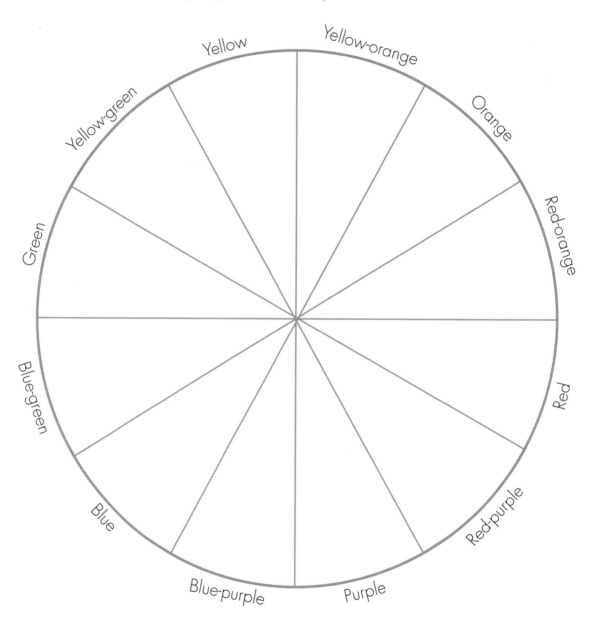

Tip: You can look back at your colour wheel at any time.

2 Colour-in the waves. You could use different shades of blue.

3 Draw lots of birds using simple shapes.

4 What is hiding in here?
Draw it behind the underwater plants.

5 Imagine what you might see through this window and draw it below. You could be looking inside or outside.

6

Design some clothes to hang on to the hangers. You could cut out shapes in paper and then add patterns in pencils or pens. You could draw tops, trousers (pants), skirts, or even socks!

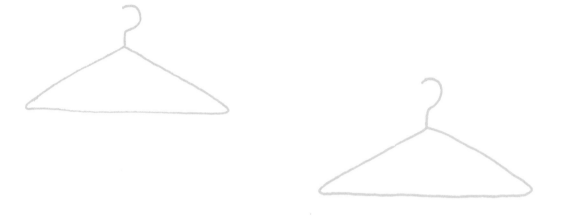

Tip: Ask a grown-up to help if you are using scissors.

7

Practise colour mixing with paint!

All you need to start is **red**, **yellow** and **blue**. These are the primary colours, and cannot be made from mixing other colours.

You can use these 3 primary colours to create secondary colours.

Primary

Secondary

Explore mixing colours. What colours can you make?

Tip: Clean your brush in water before dipping it in a new colour. This will keep your colours clean and bright!

8 Explore using white crayons (wax pastels), white paint and white pencils. What could you draw on this black background?

9 Fill this area with life. Are there plants? Animals? Birds? Insects?

10 Time for a challenge! Draw an object without looking at your page. Choose something to draw and keep your eyes on it, looking very carefully. Follow the shape with your eyes and move your pencil at the same time.

Tip: Don't worry about how your drawing looks. This activity is about learning to really look at an object, and helps your drawing skill!

11 Fill this space with stars.

 **12** Continue the diamond pattern using different art materials.

13 Draw your family!

14 Draw a tree. Use any art materials you like. Start with the trunk and branches and then add the leaves or flowers.

15 Draw the Earth from two different views. You could look at pictures, or draw from imagination.

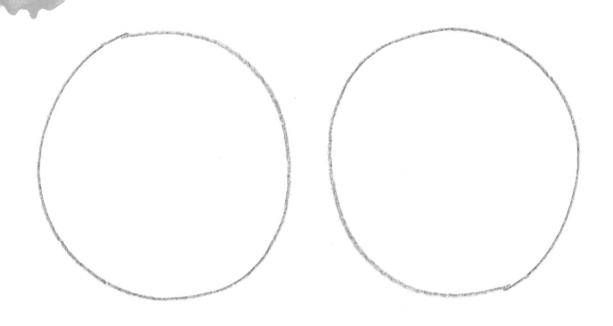

16 Fill the space with drawings of shells.
Or draw one shell with a creature living inside!

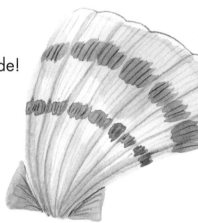

17 Enjoy filling in the diamond shapes. Choose your colours carefully. Perhaps go back and look at your colour wheel.

18 Design some badges (pins).
Are they for superheroes?

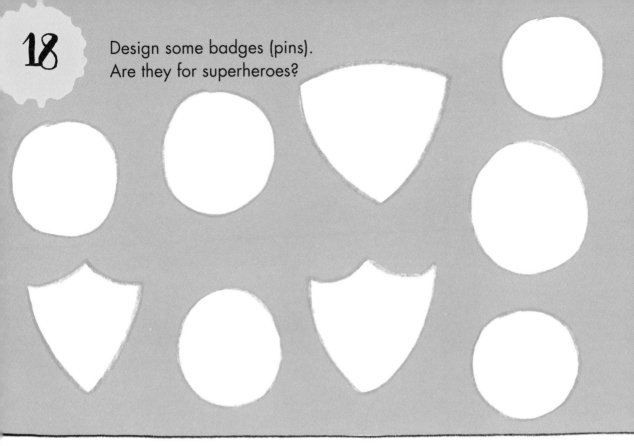

19 What is in the cups? Pencils? Flowers? Spoons?

20

Draw a portrait of yourself. Also draw things that you like. Before there were photos, important people liked to be painted surrounded by their favourite things, to show what their personality was like.

21 Explore colours that look good together. Fill in the boxes with colours that you think work well side by side.

Create a page of fields. What could be in them?

23 Make a collage of coloured circles. You could add patterns on top too.

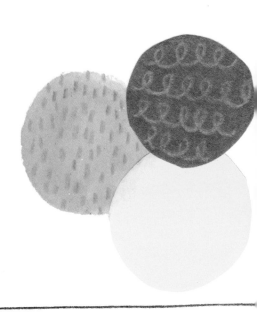

24 Continue colouring in the circles using different art materials in each circle. Try paint, coloured pencils and crayons (wax pastels).

Colour in the leaves.

26

What could the people be looking at?
It must be worth taking a photo of! Draw it.

There is symmetry in nature. Can you add patterns to these butterflies?

28 Design a pair of jumpers (sweaters).

29 Draw some ways to get around.
Cars? Trains? Bicycles? Or even a flying horse?!

30

Sit in front of a mirror and look at your reflection. Draw your face with both hands at the same time. Hold a pencil in each hand and, starting at the top of your head, draw using both pencils. Use the left side of this page to draw the left side of your reflection. Use the right side of this page to draw the right side of your reflection.

Left   *Right*

Tip: Try to keep both pencils moving at the same time!

31

Draw some boats on the water. You could cut paper to create
the shapes of the boats, and then add details with felt-tip pens.

32 Continue drawing a wiggly, loopy, black line,
then colour in the shapes using coloured pencils.

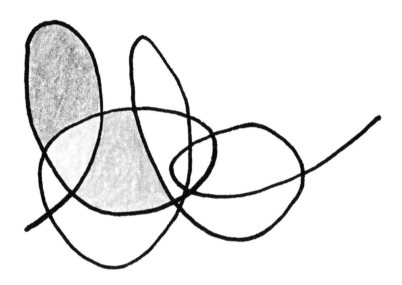

33 Fill the page with leaf shapes.
How many different shapes can you think of?

34 Create some mini abstract drawings or collages.
An abstract drawing doesn't have to look like anything real.
Have fun making marks, and playing with shape and colour.

35 Make a drawing with line and colour. Paint a plant in bold colours. Then, when the paint has dried, use a pen or coloured pencil to add detail and an outline.

1.

2.

36

Coloured paper can be used as part of your drawing.
Create a drawing that uses the blue of this paper.
You could use crayons (wax pastels) or coloured pencils,
and explore using bright colours.

37 Draw the houses.

38 Design a lampshade.

Turn these paint splodges into animals.

40 Add colour to the plants.

41 Create rainbows using different art materials and colours.

42 Fill the picture frames with artwork. Perhaps some people, scenes, or a still life?

43

Even simple things in your home can become interesting subjects and inspire art. Look at a piece of fruit, then draw it from many different views.

44 Paint something interesting that caught
your eye during your day.

45 Use the squares and grids to make patterns in each block.

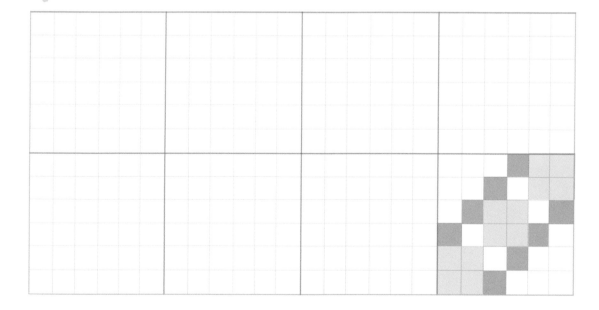

Practise drawing the features on the faces. Add hair, ears, noses, mouths, and draw the eyes about half way down the face.

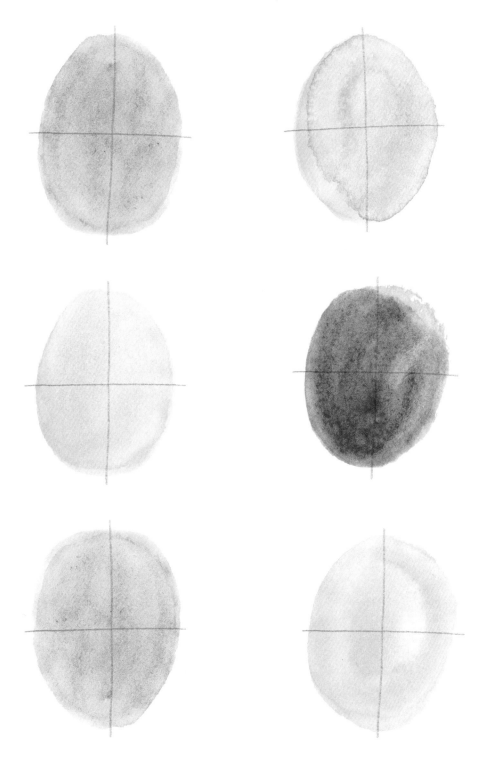

47 Draw the fish.

48

Draw the sky that you can see today.
Is it really just blue? How many different colours can you see?

49

Design two tiles. Could the patterns join up?

50

When you draw with paper you can create bold shapes. Create a drawing using just cut and torn paper. It could be an abstract image, or perhaps something from nature. Enjoy exploring shape and colour.

Tip: Play with the position of parts of your design first, before you stick it down.

51 Draw your shoes or feet.

52 Create a pattern in each of the circles.

53 Fill the page with these bumpy lines.

Tip: Move your brush slowly and steadily.

54 Mix a bit of paint and water in a palette, then dip in your finger or thumb and create fingerprints on the page. Create characters from the marks you make.

55 Draw an unusual meal you've had this week.

56 Draw the ingredients of your favourite sandwich.
It could be a sandwich you've never tried.

57 Create a mosaic using these squares. Mosaics are usually made o
small tiles, and created to decorate people's homes.

58 Museums and galleries can be interesting places to see art and historical objects. What could the people here be looking at? Draw your ideas.

59 Fill the flats with life.

Shading adds tone to your drawings. There are different ways to add shading. Try them for yourself in the boxes below.

1. Try cross-hatching with pencil. Add more lines to the areas that you'd like to look darker. The more lines in an the area, the darker it looks.

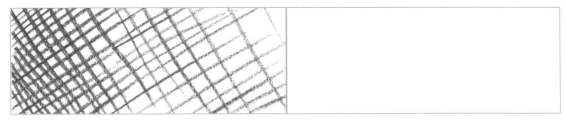

2. Using a pencil, press harder when shading the areas you'd like to be darkest. Press lightly to make an area lighter.

3. Try a felt-tip pen. Add more dots to the areas you'd like to be appear darker. The more dots you use, the darker it looks.

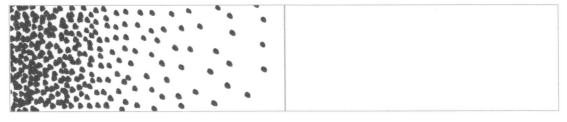

4. Try using paint. Start with a light wash of colour over the whole box, then add more layers of colour to the areas you'd like to be darkest.

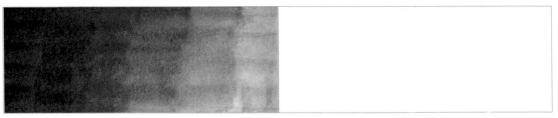

61 What could the paintbrush have just finished painting?

62 Design a wallpaper behind this chair. Perhaps the floor too!

63 Add flowers and design the vases. People have been making and designing pottery for at least 18,000 years!

 **64** Imagine this is a window that you are looking out at night-time. Draw what you might see.

65

Use coloured paper to create the sea. Carefully cut or tear strips of paper. You could draw onto the paper first using coloured pencils. Is it a calm sea? Or is it wild?

66

Fill the space with things that are the colour yellow.

67 Fill the space with painted colourful stripes.
Move your brush slowly across the page.

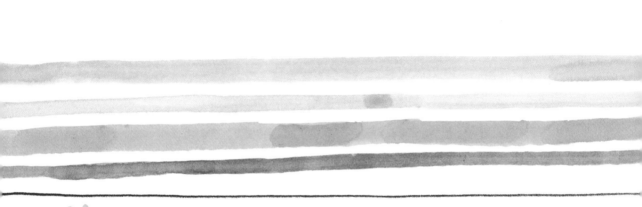

68 Fill the space with things that are the colour green.

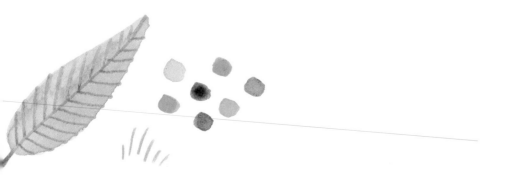

Add stripes to the bees.

70 Draw under the ground.
Perhaps there are tunnels, or hidden burrows?

71 Draw the faces of the cats.

72 Make a drawing of the flower below, using any art materials you like.

Tip: You could draw an outline first, or just go for it with colour!

73

Add colour and designs to the seahorses.
Perhaps paint the sea around them.

74 Colour in the boats.

75 Fill the space with things that are the colour orange.

Explore using different art materials together.
In each box, try to overlap at least two different materials.

Tip: You may like to look back to this page for inspiration, when choosing art materials for other activities.

77 Design a pair of t-shirts.

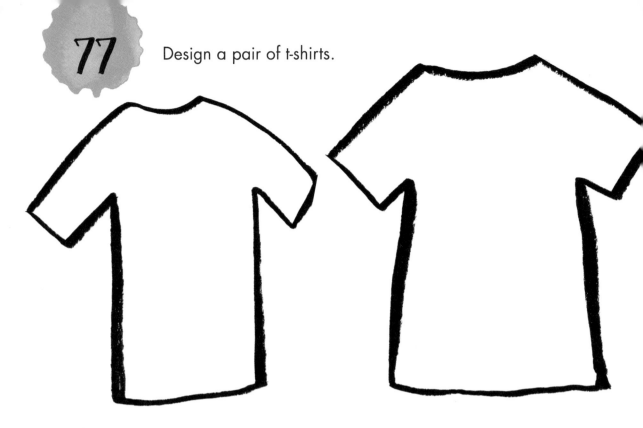

78 Fill the page with triangles to create a pattern.

Draw a friend. What could they be doing?

80

Ask a grown-up to cut a piece of fruit in half. Draw what you see using any art materials you feel like. Look carefully at the details.

 **81**

Draw an imaginary animal, made up from the parts of different animals. It could have the head of a horse, the body of a tiger, the wings of an eagle and the legs of a frog!

Fill the page with colourful beetles. People have so far discovered more than 350,000 species of beetle. There may be many more still to discover!

83 Design a pattern on the snake.

84 Complete the shoal of fish.

85 Add shadows to the bottles. Think about what direction the light is coming from. The bottles will block the suns rays.

Sun

Continue creating a pattern.

87 Design the Dala horses.
Dala horses are traditional wooden model horses from Sweden!

88 Add flowers to the stalks.

89 Practise adding tone to these cubes.
You can use any colour you like.

*Tip: Think about where
the light could be coming
from – perhaps a different
direction on each cube.
Which sides are in shadow?*

90 Design the houses in the street.

91 Fill the page with coloured dots.
What happens when you join them up?

Create patterns within the stripes. You could use cut paper, or any art material you like. Think about making bold shapes.

Colour in the wiggly lines.

 **94** Use colouring pencils to fill the space with blobs. Try blending some of the colours to see the effects.

 **95** Add trees to the forest. Could there be animals too?

Turn these paint splodges into animals.

Create a field of flowers by adding detail to these colourful blobs

Explore overlapping a variety of different art materials to create a big, wild picture!

99

Draw your colouring pencils and then colour them in.

100 Design a patterned wallpaper for this wall, and some pictures in the frames. Perhaps they are of animals, or family members.

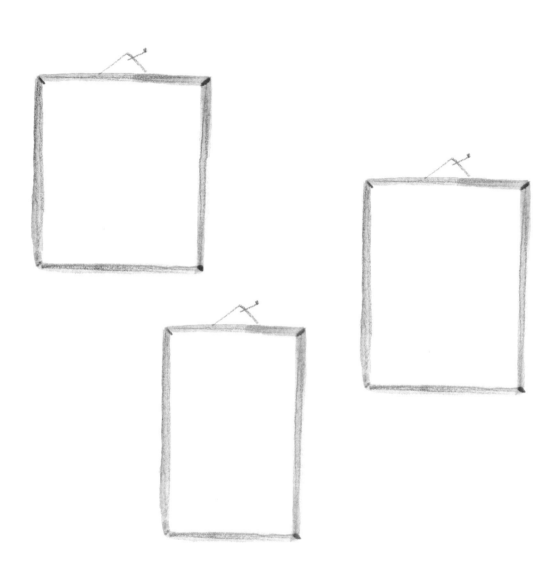

101 Turn these paint splodges into animals.

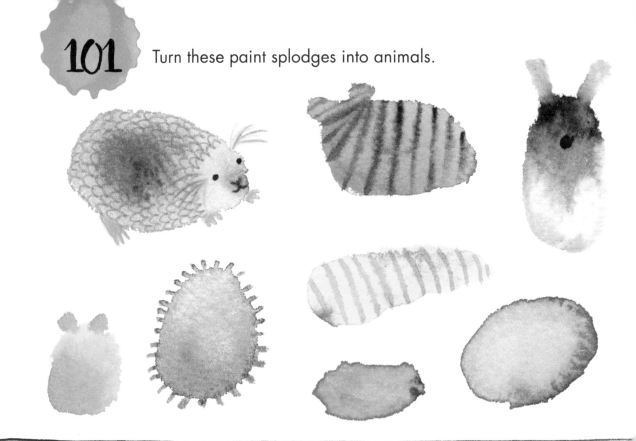

102 Create some paint splodges. What could they become?
A creature? A pattern?

103 Sit in front of a mirror and draw your reflection. Imagine that you are wearing a funny hat!

104 Explore shading and blending colours in these pears.
Try using colouring pencils in a different way for each pear.

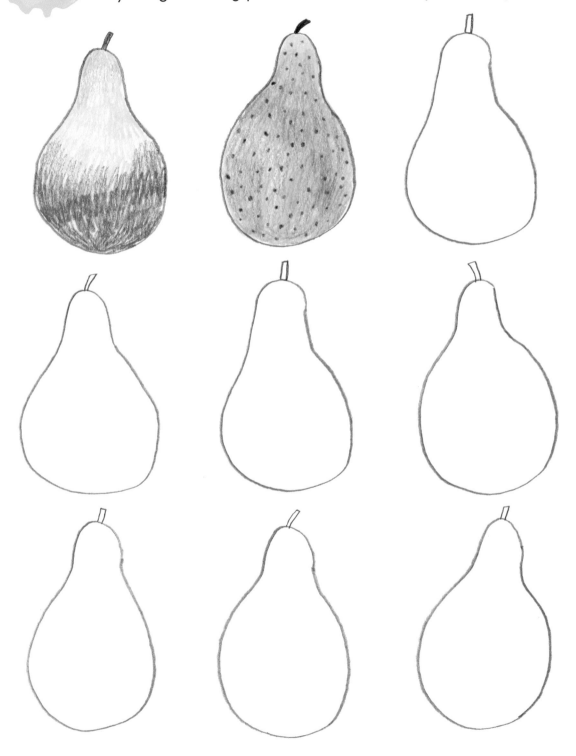

105 Continue adding to the image to create a scene full of wildlife and insects.

106 Colour the circles. You could try using different art materials like paint, cut paper and colouring pencils.

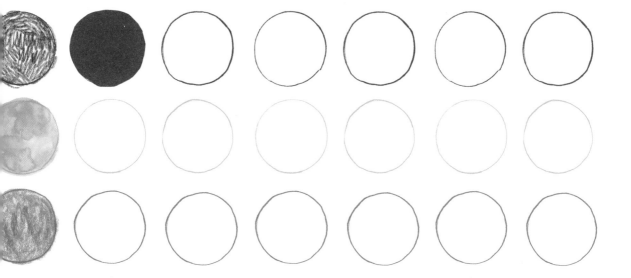

107 What can you store in the bowls? Draw something different in each one. Perhaps food, a collection of marbles, a toy?

Add patterns and petals to these flower shapes.
You could use cut paper, or any other material you like.

109 Fill each section with a different pattern.

Tip: You may like to look back to your colo
wheel to see which colours look good togeth

110 What do you think the scene would be around this slow, meandering river?

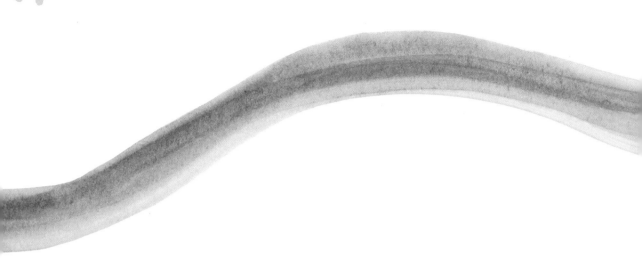

111 Design some bunting.

112 Add your own ideas to the drawing. The tree could be full of leaves, fruit, or even birds!

What interesting things can be stored in jars? Draw them.

114 Create an animal by making a collage of cut paper. Could you make stripes? Or spots?

115 A *Trompe-l'œil* drawing creates an optical illusion. Carry on drawing squiggles to trick your eye into seeing a 3D shape!

116 What might be under this light? Perhaps it's someone sneaking about, or someone just reading a book. Use your imagination.

117

What unusual things might these people
have spotted in this jungle?

118

Draw something from nature that you've seen today.
Was it outside the house, or inside?

Draw and paint your own coral to add to the reef.

120 Add colour to these starfish.

121 Continue creating your own patterns using cool colours.

Turn these splodges into cats and dogs!

123 Create a jungle. What might you fill it with?

Tip: Allow the trees and plants to overlap to make the jungle seem more wild!

124 Draw the people in your home. Try to capture the personality of each person by thinking about what they are doing in your picture.

125 Draw ten objects that you remember from your day. Try to do this from memory.

Create a repeat pattern using these instructions.

1. Draw a simple object

2. Draw the object a few times, keeping an even space between each drawing. Each drawing does not need to be perfect.

3. Add more details to achieve your repeat pattern.

127 Create your own patterns using warm colours.

128 Colour in the feathers.

129 An object looks smaller the further away it is from you. Create a picture which shows perspective. Draw a row of trees within the grey lines, to show that some of them are close and some are in the distance.

Use this rough guide to draw a face in profile (from the side). As a guide, the eyes are half way between the top of the head and the chin.

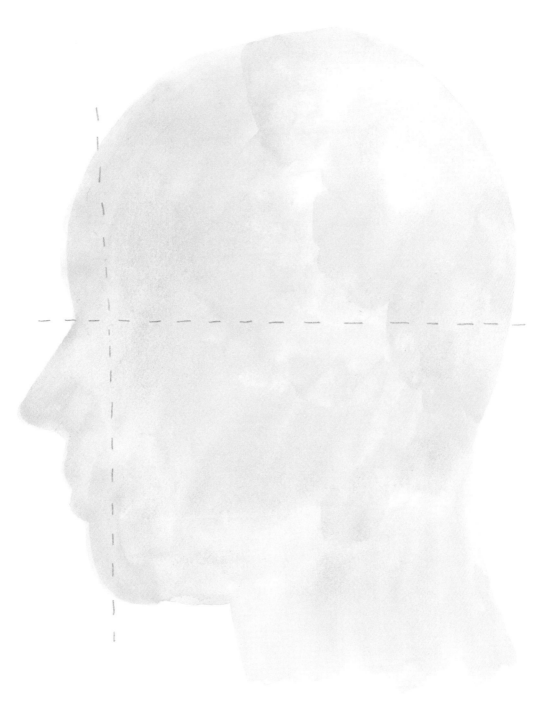

131 Add patterns to these irregular shapes.

132 You could collect pebbles and paint designs onto them.
Draw some ideas onto the stones here.

133 Design a superhero! What is their power?

134 Continue the pattern by cutting coloured paper into squares. Add patterns or designs to the boxes.

135 Draw a bang!

136 Add birds to the lines. I wonder if the birds always live in the same place, or if they migrate from far away?

137 Fill the wheel with colour using any art materials you like. Consider which colours may look good next to each other.

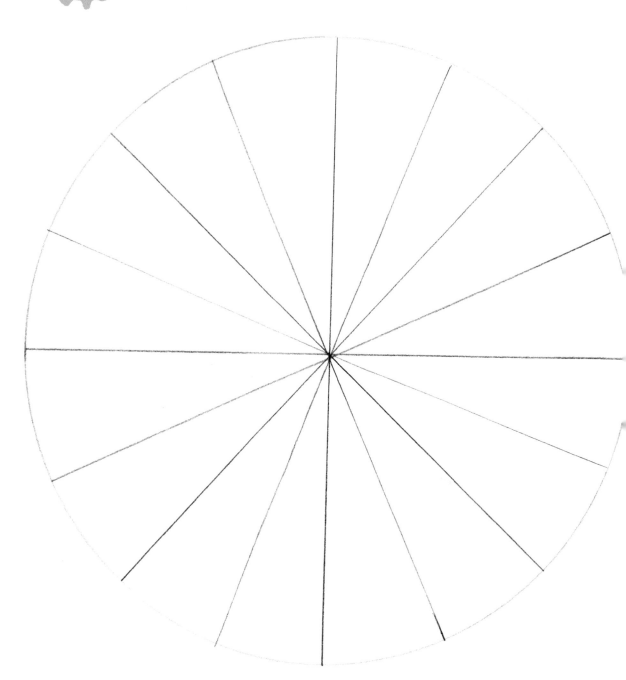

138 Explore the different effects you can create with your art materials. This will help you learn about them, and how you can have fun using them. Use the page below to make marks and lines with all your different colours and materials.

139 Add designs to the socks.

140 Use a variety of art materials to colour each of the grapes.

141 Add flower heads to the bunch of stems.

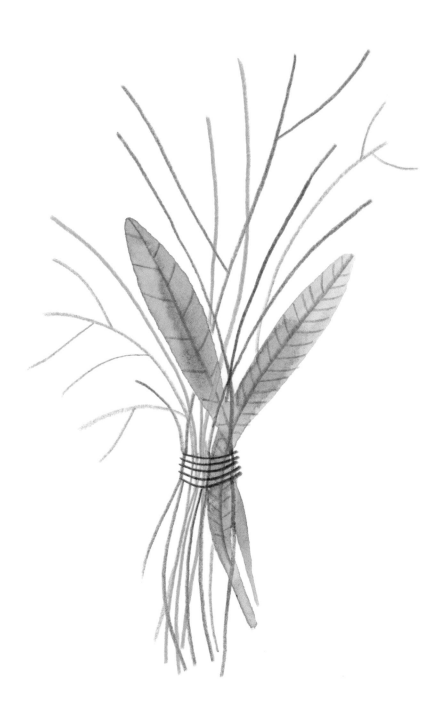

142

Create a flock of imaginary birds of paradise by adding wings, tail feathers, beaks and legs.

143 Add designs to the vases – some simple, some complex.

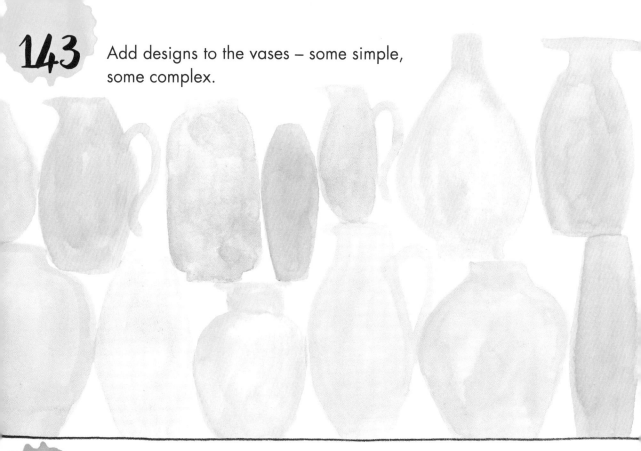

144 Add leaves to the trees. What season is it?

Draw what you might find stored in these bottles.

146 Design some party balloons.

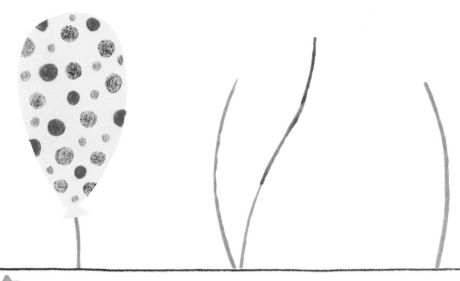

147 Continue adding zigzags to the pattern.

148 Add colour to these leaves.

149 Design three clocks.

150 Add smiley faces to the circles!

Fill the page with coloured triangles.

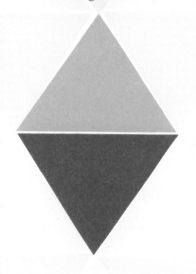

152

What might you find under the waves? Draw it here.
Are there fish? Perhaps a hidden treasure chest!

153

Draw the creature which has made these prints.

154 Create designs on the mugs (cups).

155 Turn these blobs into cacti and plants.
You could add details like exotic flowers, pots, insects and birds.

156 Add faces and hair to the crowd of people.

157 Fill the page with imaginary plants.

158 Fill the pot with art materials.
Perhaps paint brushes, felt-tip pens, and coloured pencils?

159

Using colouring pencils, carefully colour in the shapes so that where they overlap they create a new colour.

Tip: You may need to add a few layers of each colour.

160 Lots of vegetables grow beneath the ground. Draw some here, or create your own from imagination!

161 Design some cupcakes!

 Paint a design or mini picture in each coloured rectangle.

163 Draw the other half of this leaf.

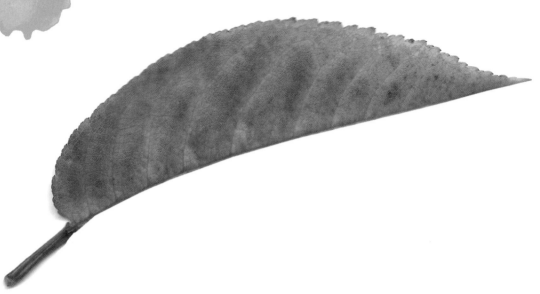

Tip: You may like to use colouring pencils as you can blend them together.

164 Continue drawing the waves.
Is there somebody snorkelling?

 **165** Carefully draw lots of rain drops.
You could draw the top of an umbrella too!

 **166** Fill the space with drawings of butterflies.

167 Add plants to the pots.

168 Draw and write a postcard that you've always wanted to send.

169   Draw your favourite toy.

---

170   Continue the leaf pattern.

171 Colour in these leaves using warm colours.

172 Add plants to the pots.

Fill the squares with concentric circles.

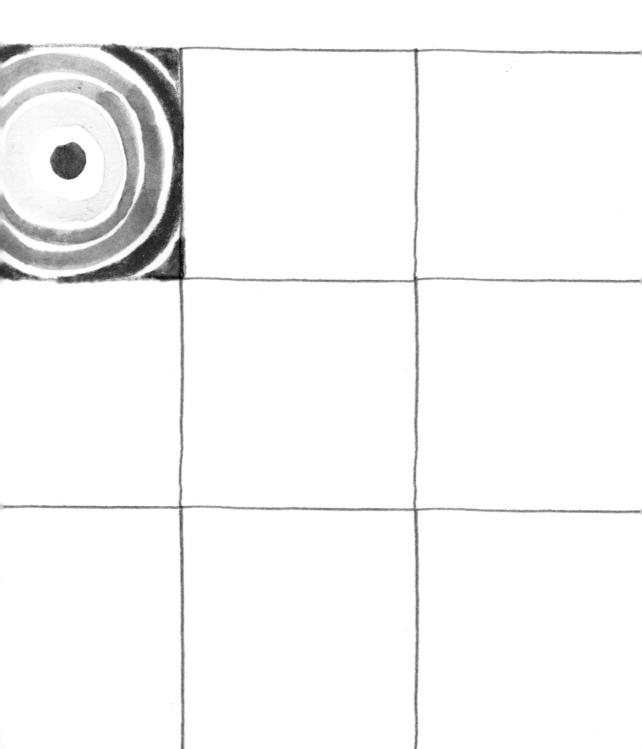

174 Draw a herd of animals in the forest clearing.

175 Colour in the circles.

176 Design an imaginary animal.

Draw what the people are looking at. Could it be some animals? Or a mythical beast? Or a dinosaur?

Add colour to these fish.

179

Fill the squares with different marks. You could try dashes, lines, spots, swirls and crosshatches.

Turn the splodges into wild animals.

181

Add tone to this sphere using colouring pencils. Follow the curve of the sphere, pressing harder as you move to the parts of the sphere that would be darkest.

Tip: Think about where the light might hit the sphere.

Fill the vase with flowers. You could cut
the petals out of coloured paper.

183 Create a rainbow!

Red

Orange

Yellow

Green

Blue

Indigo

Violet

184 Draw what is on the shelf. Books? Plants? Games?

185 Draw a tin can or packet of food from your kitchen.

186 Continue creating circles in any art material you like.

Complete this flock of birds

188 Continue the pattern. Try using different art materials.

189 Add flowers.

Bring the black splodges to life by using white crayons (wax pastels) or white colouring pencils.

191 Draw something that makes you happy.

192 Draw the animal these hooves belong to.

Create your own desert islands!

194 Find a photo of a face. Turn it upside down, and draw it here. When we look at an image upside down, it can be easier to draw it because instead of drawing what we think a face should look like, we draw what we actually see.

Tip: Your finished drawing will be upside down, so when you'e finished, turn the book to see it.

195 Use each square to experiment with making colourful patterns.

Fill the page with lines in all your favourite colours.

197

Create a drawing using collaged paper. You could draw anything that inspires you, or a whole scene!

Tip: You could use colouring pencils to add detail to your paper shapes.

198

If you could design your dream garden, what would you include? Some people trim their hedges into the shape of animals and other interesting shapes! This is called topiary.

199 Fill the page with all the fruit and vegetables you can think of.

200 Draw the flamingoes in the water. When a flamingo is relaxing or sleeping, it stands on one leg!

About the Author

Lorna Scobie grew up in the English countryside, climbing trees and taking her rabbit for walks in the fields. She is an illustrator and book designer, now based in London.

Lorna draws every day, and always has a sketchbook on her when she's out and about, just in case.

If you'd like to keep up to date with Lorna's work, she can be found on Instagram and Twitter: **@lornascobie**

www.lornascobie.com

For Isla

Published in 2020 by Hardie Grant Books,
an imprint of Hardie Grant Publishing

Hardie Grant Books (London)
5th & 6th Floors
52–54 Southwark Street
London SE1 1UN

Hardie Grant Books (Melbourne)
Building 1, 658 Church Street
Richmond, Victoria 3121

hardiegrantbooks.com

British Library Cataloguing-in-Publication Data.
A catalogue record for this book is available
from the British Library.

Art at Home
ISBN: 978-1-78488-400-0

Publishing Director: Kate Pollard
Commissioning Editor: Kajal Mistry
Illustrations: Lorna Scobie

Colour Reproduction by p2d
Printed and bound in China by Leo Paper Products Ltd.